Hurricanes

by Kate Boehm Jerome

sundance™

sundance™
A Haights Cross Communications Company

Program written and developed by Kate Boehm Jerome
in association with Sundance Publishing.

Editorial, Design, and Production by Baseline Development Group
in association with Sundance Publishing.

Consultant/Reviewer: Rebecca L. Johnson, Science Writer, Sioux Falls, SD

Published by
Sundance Publishing
P.O. Box 740
One Beeman Road
Northborough, MA 01532-0740
800-343-8204
www.sundancepub.com

Photography:
Cover AP/Wide World Photos; p. 1 © DANIEL AGUILAR/Reuters/CORBIS; p. 3 AP/Wide World Photos; pp. 4-5 © Mike Theiss/Jim Reed Photography/CORBIS; p. 6 Tony Craddock/Photo Researchers, Inc.; p. 8 © Greg Probst/CORBIS; p. 9 (top left, bottom left, right) Photodisc/Getty Images; p. 11 DOC/NOAA/NWS/NCEP/Hydrometeorological Prediction Center; p. 12 © Dynamic Graphics Group/IT Stock Free/Alamy; p. 13 © DANIEL AGUILAR/Reuters/CORBIS; p. 16 © Royalty-Free/CORBIS; p. 17 World Perspectives/Getty Images; pp. 18-19 © Dorling Kindersley/DKimages.com; p. 20 © Warren Faidley/CORBIS; p. 21 AP/Wide World Photos; p. 22 Stock Connection/fotosearch.com; p. 23 (all) National Oceanic & Atmospheric Administration (NOAA); p. 24 © Jim Reed/CORBIS; p. 25 (left) © Royalty-Free/CORBIS, (right) © Erik S. Lesser/epa/CORBIS; p. 27 AP/Wide World Photos; (top) p. 29 Tony Craddock/Photo Researchers, Inc.

Illustration:
pp. 10, 14-15 Wendy Smith

ISBN-13: 978-1-4207-0335-1
ISBN-10: 1-4207-0335-8

Printed in China

Cover photo: Hurricane Katrina hits Miami, Florida

Table of Contents

Real Ocean Monsters

The year 2005 was a very bad year for hurricanes. A monster storm named Hurricane Katrina severely damaged the Gulf Coast states of Alabama, Mississippi, and Louisiana. Three weeks later, another strong storm, Hurricane Rita, hit Florida, Louisiana, and Texas. Twenty-seven tropical storms formed during the 2005 Atlantic hurricane season, and fifteen of them turned into hurricanes. It was a new record—and one that came with a very high cost. More than a thousand people lost their lives, and billions of dollars of damage took place.

So how do such monster storms form out in the ocean? To understand hurricanes, you first have to start with a few basics about the weather.

CHAPTER 1

It All Starts with the Sun

You've heard it a hundred times before. The sun is the major source of energy on Earth. So it should be no surprise to you to learn that it's the sun's energy that powers our weather.

Air Temperature

Believe it or not, sunlight passing through the air is not what heats the air. So how does air warm up? Sunlight warms the surface of the earth. Then the surface of the earth warms the air above it.

But there's a catch. Sunlight doesn't warm the earth evenly in all places. Since the earth's surface is curved, the sun's rays strike the earth at different angles. The North and South Poles get the most indirect sunlight, so their surfaces stay the coldest. The equator gets the most direct sunlight, so the surface of the earth around the equator stays the warmest.

This means there is lots of warm air over the tropical oceans near the equator—and that's exactly what hurricanes need. In fact, all **hurricanes** begin over the tropical oceans of the world.

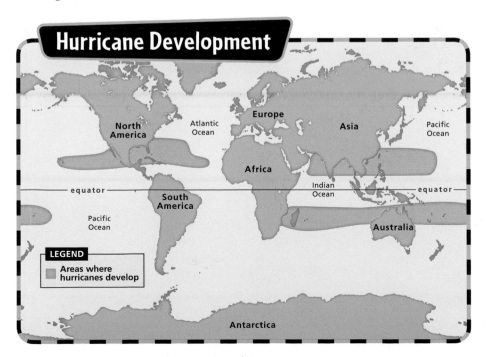

Hurricane Development

North America
Atlantic Ocean
Europe
Asia
Pacific Ocean
Africa
equator
South America
Indian Ocean
equator
Pacific Ocean
Australia

LEGEND
■ Areas where hurricanes develop

Antarctica

But let's get back to the uneven warming of air. Even in areas that get the same angle of sunlight, different surfaces of the earth absorb different amounts of light energy. This means some surfaces warm up faster than others. Look at the picture on this page. On a sunny summer day, the land heats up faster than the ocean next to it. This means the air above the land will warm faster than the air above the ocean.

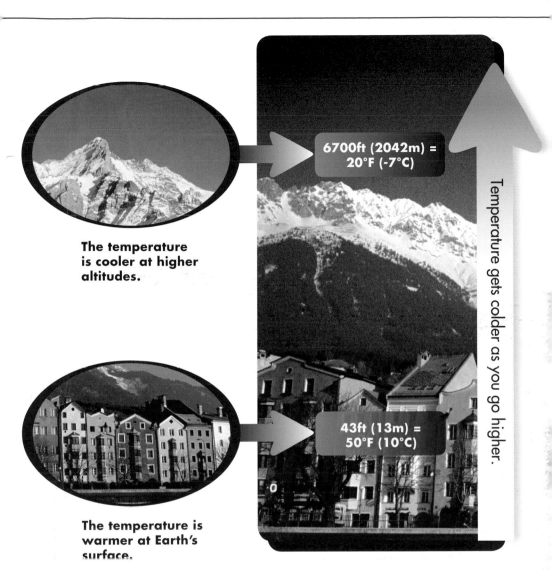

The temperature is cooler at higher altitudes.

6700ft (2042m) = 20°F (-7°C)

43ft (13m) = 50°F (10°C)

Temperature gets colder as you go higher.

The temperature is warmer at Earth's surface.

One more thing you should know is that air temperature changes as you go higher above the earth. This makes sense if you think about how the air is heated in the first place. It's the earth's surface that heats the air. So the higher up you go and the farther away you get from the earth's surface, the colder the air gets.

Air Pressure

So what do changing air temperatures have to do with weather? Well, differences in air temperature cause air to move. As air gets warmer, its particles move farther apart. This makes warm air lighter than cold air. So warm air rises and cold air sinks.

Differences in air temperature also affect **air pressure.** What's air pressure? It's the weight of the air that is constantly pressing down on you and everything else on Earth. Like air temperature, air pressure can change.

Moving Air

Cold Air Sinking

Warm Air Rising

LEGEND

Cold Air

Warm Air

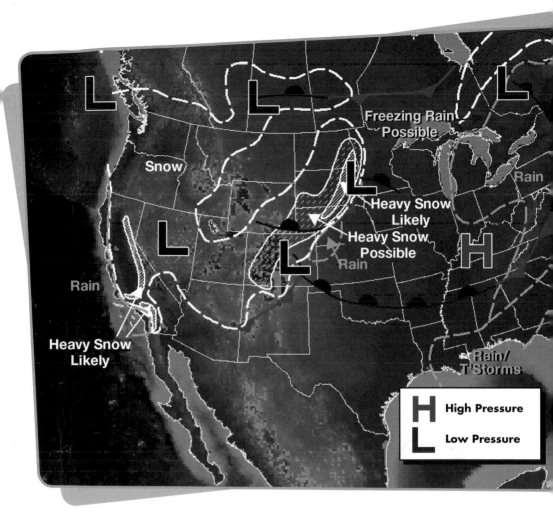

When warmer, lighter air rises, it pushes down
on the surface of the earth with less pressure. So a
low pressure area forms beneath the warm air.

Cold air is heavier than warm air. So it tends to
sink and push down on the earth's surface with more
pressure. This causes a **high pressure area** to form.
Areas of high pressure and low pressure are often
shown on daily weather maps.

Wind

Now here's the important part. Air moves from an area of high pressure to an area of low pressure. When air moves, you get wind!

Have you ever felt a sea breeze? It's the wind that blows from the ocean onto the shore. On a hot, sunny day, the ocean heats more slowly than the land. This makes the air above the water cooler. It also creates an area of high pressure. Since air moves from high pressure to low pressure, the wind blows from the ocean to the shore.

As air moves across the ocean and onto the land, it forms a sea breeze that blows this blanket.

Hurricane force winds can damage trees and blow down signs.

On a very blustery day, the wind may gust to 30 miles
(48 kilometers) per hour. This type of wind can blow
your hat off or turn your umbrella inside out. Although
it may be annoying, this much wind is usually not
life-threatening.

The winds in a hurricane, however, can gust to
over 200 miles (about 322 kilometers) per hour. Objects
that are light weight, such as lawn chairs, become
dangerous missiles when they are hurtled through the
air by such strong winds. Even strong steel structures
can bend or break in hurricane winds. It's no wonder
these storms can cause such damage.

The Water Cycle

So now we've figured out wind, but what about the clouds? Again, it all goes back to the sun. That's because the sun's energy fuels a 24/7 process called the **water cycle.** And clouds form during the water cycle.

Here's how it works. Water **evaporates** from the earth's surface and is changed into **water vapor** that mixes with the air. Water vapor is water in the form of a gas.

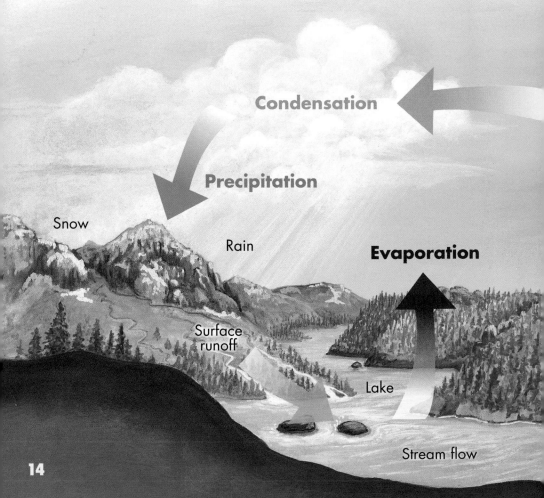

Condensation

Precipitation

Snow

Rain

Evaporation

Surface runoff

Lake

Stream flow

Warm air rising above the earth eventually starts to cool. This makes water vapor change, or **condense,** into tiny drops of liquid water or ice crystals. When millions of tiny drops or crystals group together, a cloud is formed.

When the drops or crystals in a cloud get large and heavy enough, water returns to the earth as rain or snow. As you know, this is called **precipitation.**

Condensation

Evaporation

Ocean

BLUE PLANET Note

When the air feels hot and "sticky," you are feeling the water vapor in it. Air with lots of water vapor has high **humidity.** High temperatures and high humidity combine to create a high **heat index,** which can make you feel hotter than the actual temperature outside.

CHAPTER 2

Hurricane Central

Now that you've got the basics, let's move on to the hurricane itself! As the tropics begin to heat up in the summer, lots of warm, moist air rises from the ocean. This can cause large thunderstorms to form.

Hurricane eye

The eye of a hurricane is calm compared to the strong winds in the eyewall around it.

BLUE PLANET Note

Although hurricanes can form at any time, the official hurricane season in the Atlantic Ocean falls between June 1 and November 30.

If wind and temperature conditions are just right, these thunderstorms can start to cluster together. If enough thunderstorms join together, then a tropical storm forms.

Sometimes a tropical storm continues to grow. Once the winds of a tropical storm reach 74 miles (119 kilometers) per hour, it officially becomes a hurricane.

When you look at a picture of a hurricane taken from high above it, you can usually see huge bands of clouds swirling around an open circle, called the **eye.** The eye of a hurricane is surprisingly calm, with little wind. But the area surrounding the eye, or the **eyewall,** is the most dangerous part of the storm. This is where the hurricane winds are at their strongest.

The Energy Machine

Hurricanes can be really big. A typical storm can be 300 miles (about 483 kilometers) wide. A monster storm can stretch for thousands of miles.

So how does a hurricane keep itself going?
A hurricane needs the right wind conditions and warm ocean water to keep growing. Although hurricanes form under big areas of high pressure, the warm, moist air inside a hurricane creates an area of low pressure. As warm air rises, air near the ocean rushes into this low pressure area to replace it. The water vapor in the warm, rising air then cools and condenses. This releases more heat and forms more clouds. If the upper level winds don't blow these clouds apart, the storm can get bigger.

Remember, the warm ocean water is the constant source of fuel that keeps the hurricane going. If the hurricane moves over colder water or land, it loses its source of energy and begins to fall apart.

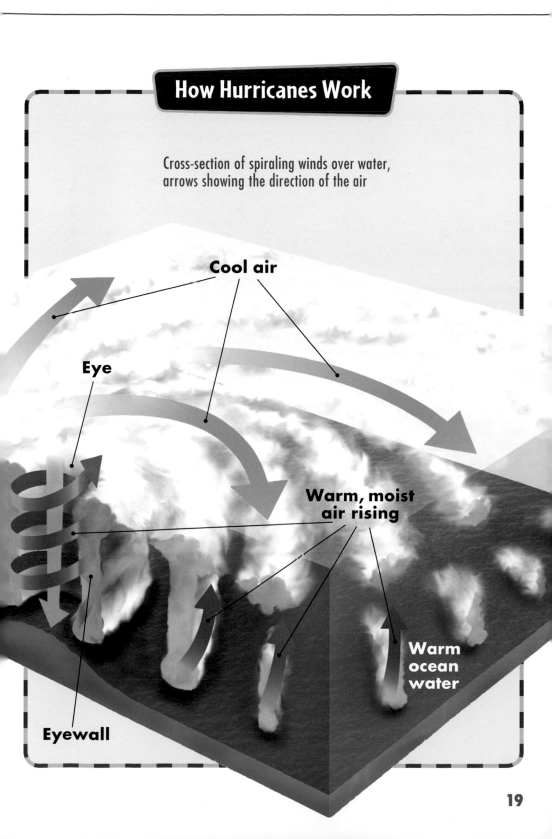

How Hurricanes Work

Cross-section of spiraling winds over water,
arrows showing the direction of the air

Cool air

Eye

Warm, moist
air rising

Warm
ocean
water

Eyewall

Dangerous Floodwaters

You know that hurricane winds can be life-threatening and cause great damage. But the most widespread loss of life in a hurricane comes from another problem. It's the floodwaters.

The most immediate flood danger to coastal areas occurs when a hurricane first comes ashore. The surface of the sea is actually sucked up under the low pressure system of a hurricane. This forms a big bulge of water, or **storm surge,** under the hurricane. If the hurricane comes ashore during high tide, when the water is already rising, the storm surge can be even bigger. The high winds of a hurricane also whip up huge waves. When it all comes together, a big hurricane can hit land with a wall of water up to 20 feet (6 meters) high. Most of the coastal areas along the Gulf of Mexico and the southeastern United States are only 10 feet (3 meters) above sea level. So a huge storm surge can put everything underwater.

A 15-foot storm surge flooded the town of Mobile, Alabama, in 2005.

Residents of Gulfport, Mississippi, had to paddle through their neighborhood after Hurricane Katrina flooded the streets.

And it's not just the coastal areas that suffer! Hurricanes moving inland can still pack a punch. **Tornadoes** sometimes spring up as an offshoot of the storm. Soaking rains fill rivers and streams until they overflow their banks.

In 2005, Hurricane Katrina caused enormous damage along the coastal areas of Alabama, Louisiana, and Mississippi. But the destruction did not stop at the coast. Katrina brought floodwaters six miles inland from the Mississippi coast. And as the storm moved northward, at least three tornadoes were reported in Georgia—a whole state away.

BLUE PLANET Note

Tropical storm or hurricane names usually begin with one of 21 letters from the alphabet. However, since 2005 had 27 storms, six letters of the Greek alphabet (Alpha, Beta, Gamma, Delta, Epsilon, and Zeta) had to be used as names for the first time.

21

CHAPTER 3

Staying Safe

So what's the first thing people need in order to stay safe when a hurricane threatens? Good information! Weather satellites provide some of that data. Weather experts use this information as they build computer models to track an approaching storm.

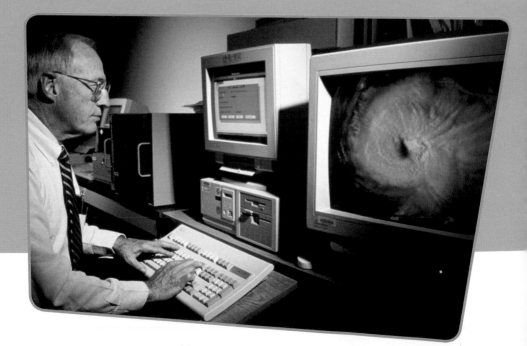

Hurricane Hunters

The skilled men and women who are known as hurricane hunters actually fly big airplanes right into the middle of monster storms to get a bird's-eye view of what's going on. They gather information about such things as wind speed, rainfall, and air pressure. **The National Hurricane Center** in Florida uses this data to predict how big the hurricane might get and where it might move.

How come a hurricane that is strong enough to destroy a house doesn't damage a hurricane hunter's airplane? It all has to do with how these planes are built.

For example, large C-130 turboprop planes are shaped so that air can easily flow around them. Houses, on the other hand, are built to stand still—not move. Their flat walls and tall roof take the full force of the hurricane.

BLUE PLANET Note

Sometimes the rain and clouds are so heavy in a hurricane that the crew can barely see the wings on their own airplane.

C-130 turboprop plane

U.S. DEPT. OF COMMERCE

NOAA 41C

Staying Ahead of the Storm

Once it looks like a hurricane is going to hit land, the National Hurricane Center sends out alerts. When a hurricane is 36 hours away from making landfall, a hurricane watch is issued. This means people in the watch area need to start securing their property against the storm. It also means they need to have a plan in case they need to leave the area.

People board up their windows at home and at work to prepare for hurricanes.

Time to move! When a hurricane is only 24 hours from making landfall, a hurricane warning is posted. By this time, forecasters are usually more certain of the path of the hurricane. But it is still very difficult to pinpoint the exact area where the storm might hit. A hurricane warning usually means people have to **evacuate,** or leave, the coastal areas closest to the ocean.

Evacuation sign

EVACUATION ROUTE

Hurricane evacuations can lead to traffic jams on major highways.

A Brighter Future

Scientists rate hurricanes in five categories. A Category One hurricane causes the least damage; a Category Five causes the most damage.

The chart below describes the different ratings. These ratings give people an idea of how bad the flooding and property damage might be with each category, or size of storm. It also helps them make decisions about evacuating before the storm hits.

Saffir-Simpson Hurricane Scale

Hurricane Rating	Hurricane Speed	Potential Damage
Category 1 Hurricane	winds 74 to 95 mph	Little damage to buildings, shrubs, and trees.
Category 2 Hurricane	winds 96 to 110 mph	Some trees blown down. Some damage to roofs, doors, and windows.
Category 3 Hurricane	winds 111 to 130 mph	Large trees blown down. Some walls collapse. Flooding along coast destroys small buildings.
Category 4 Hurricane	winds 131 to 155 mph	Mobile homes completely destroyed. Major damage to doors and windows. Some inland flooding.
Category 5 Hurricane	winds 156 mph and up	Roofs totally destroyed on many homes and businesses. All trees and road signs blown down.

New bridge

Old bridge

A new cable-stay bridge over the Cooper River in South Carolina has been built to withstand hurricane winds of around 190 miles (306 kilometers) per hour.

But there's still a lot to do! Scientists are constantly working on ways to improve their hurricane path predictions. Technology helps a lot. For example, new radar delivers more information in a faster way. This helps create more accurate computer models.

Engineers are also in the mix. They work to improve building materials. This allows new houses and bridges to be built in ways that will help them withstand even greater wind speeds and flood conditions. We may not be able to stop a hurricane's fury, but we can keep trying to find new ways to protect ourselves.

And who knows? Perhaps one day you will be the one to make a major breakthrough that keeps people safer when a monster hurricane strikes!

Blue Planet E-Diary Blog

Tuesday: Writing Assignment

Extra! Extra!
Read all about it!

From magazines and newspapers, to Internet and TV, it's no wonder this is called the Information Age! Where do you get your information from?

You've been hired to write a short newspaper article on hurricanes. The headline for your article is:

Hurricanes: The Facts Behind the Fury

While you write your article, think about what you now know. What do you need to say to help people understand these monster storms? Try to explain what hurricanes are, how they form, and why they can be dangerous.

posted by BluePlanetXpert / 3:45 PM / Comments 0

Instant Message

Subject:
It starts in the tropics!

>**sunray:** Where do hurricanes develop?

BluePlanetXpert: Since hurricanes depend on warm air, the tropical oceans near the equator are the perfect place for them to develop.

>**sunray:** How do they move?

BluePlanetXpert: Hurricanes feed off of warm waters and are propelled by strong winds. Wind currents that surround the storm determine the direction in which the storm will move.

Blue Planet Chat Room

Subject:
Extra! Extra!

>**sunray:** Have you ever seen a hurricane?

stormtrack: No, I grew up in Minnesota.

beachbum1: We got caught in one while we were in Jamaica! We had to evacuate the hotel.

cloudburst: I've only seen pictures on TV.

Glossary

air pressure the weight of air that is constantly pressing down on everything on Earth

condense when water vapor cools and changes from a gas into a liquid

evacuate to leave an area in an organized fashion to keep safe

evaporates when water warms enough to change from a liquid to a gas

eye the calm area in the center of a hurricane

eyewall the ring of thunderstorms that surrounds a hurricane's eye, containing the heaviest rain and the strongest winds

heat index measure of humidity and temperature that indicates how warm you will feel outside

humidity the amount of water vapor in the air

high pressure area a place where cool air sinks and pushes down on the earth's surface with more pressure

hurricanes huge storms with very high winds that form over a tropical ocean

low pressure area a place where warm air rises and pushes down on the earth with less pressure

National Hurricane Center U.S. federal agency located in south Florida that is responsible for forecasting tropical storms and hurricanes

precipitation water that falls from the sky as rain, sleet, snow, or hail

storm surge the huge mass of water pushed onto land when a hurricane first makes landfall

tornadoes violent storms occurring over land that have a funnel-shaped cloud extending to the ground

water cycle a process in which water is constantly moved between the earth's surface and the atmosphere

water vapor water in the form of a gas

Index